AF316605

WHY DO WE NEED MONEY?

Technology for Kids

Children's Reference & Nonfiction

In this book, we're going to talk about why we need money, and how money has transformed as technology changes. So, let's get right to it!

Money didn't always exist. In the early part of human civilization, people used a system of trade to get the things they needed. This barter system allowed them to offer something they had, for something else that they needed.

PODUNK WEEKLY BUGLE.
2.5 lb. BLACK BASS. CAUGHT BY Dr. JO PARKER.
HARPERS WEEKLY
JOURNAL OF CIVILIZATION
"TOO THIN"
CHURCH
Barter

For example, if you were a farmer and had a dozen eggs, you may have offered them to the baker in exchange for a loaf of freshly baked bread. At the beginning, money was used for objects people needed to survive, such as food, tools, and medicine. However, as civilizations became more sophisticated, money was also used for luxury items.

In a way, plants and animals use systems of "bartering" too. For example, pilot fish clean harmful parasites off sharks and the sharks in return offer protection for the pilot fish. Pilot fish even travel into sharks' mouths without any fear that the shark will eat them.

THE DISADVANTAGES OF BARTERING

There were quite a few problems with bartering. First of all, some things that you wanted to exchange might have been difficult to carry around. Suppose you wanted to offer a cow in exchange for four pigs. It wouldn't be easy to take your cow over to the next town to make that barter happen.

Secondly, you couldn't easily divide up the items you were bartering, even if your buyer agreed with you on the price. For example, suppose the villager in the next town wanted to buy your cow but he only had two pigs. You couldn't sell him half a cow, so the exchange wouldn't happen.

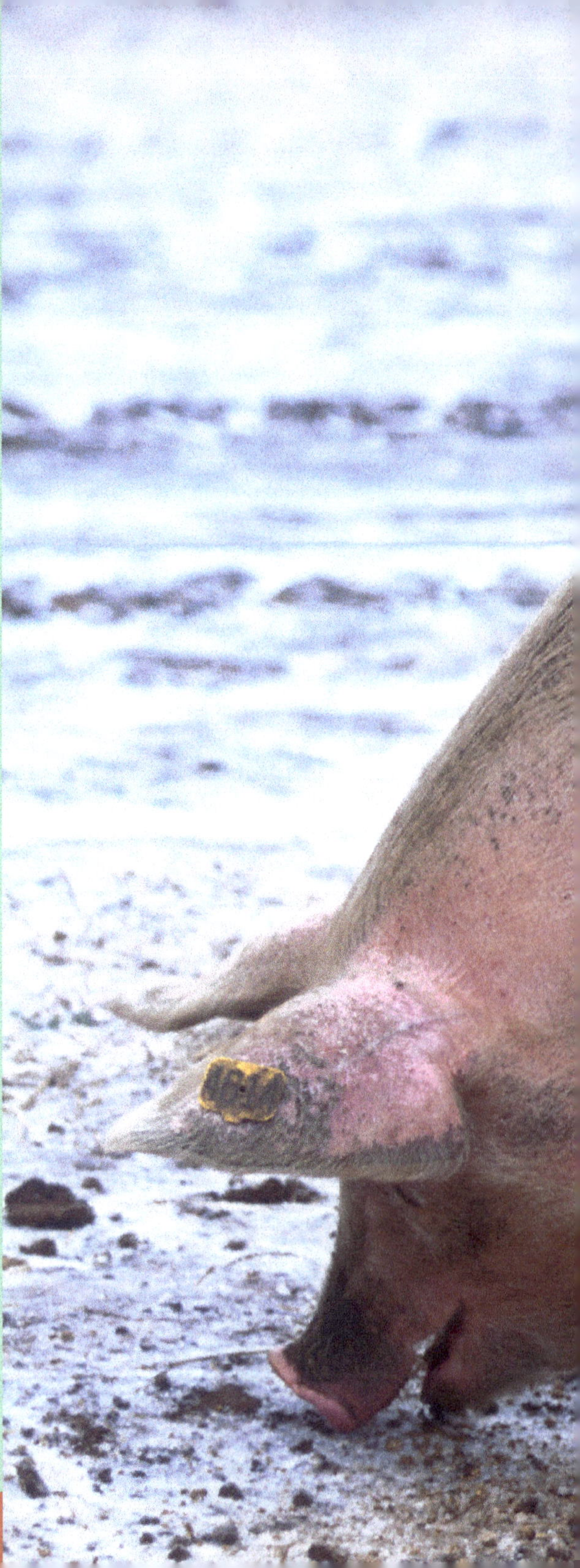

Another scenario would be if you wanted to sell the cow, but couldn't agree on the exchange rate. Maybe you think your cow should be exchanged for four pigs but a second villager you're trying to barter with only thinks your cow is worth three pigs. Many ancient disputes probably happened from heated arguments about the value of different items offered for barter.

Another problem was with items that didn't stay fresh or edible for long. If you were taking fresh fruit to market, by the time you sold them they might not have been worth what they were worth when you first picked them off the tree!

All these problems with bartering meant that people had to devise a better way to purchase the things that they needed and wanted. Money was soon invented in different forms. Even though barter still exists, most civilizations quickly converted to systems of money to buy and sell objects and services.

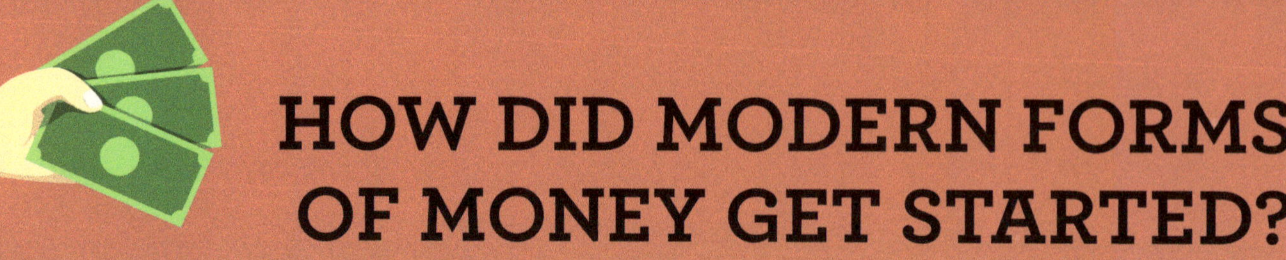

HOW DID MODERN FORMS OF MONEY GET STARTED?

No one knows for certain exactly when the first human being got the idea for money. The idea was rather complicated. Money stood for a specific value. For example, if you have a twenty-dollar bill that your dad has given you for cleaning out the garage, that twenty-dollar bill doesn't have value in and of itself. It's simply a piece of paper.

Paper money represents a specific value. That value would also stay stable, at least for a period of time. For example, you know approximately how many groceries you could buy with it, and if you go to the store two months in a row, what you could buy wouldn't change very much. However, if you had that same twenty-dollar bill and went to the store in 1930, you could have bought a lot more with it.

After bartering was used, the next stage of the evolution of money was when standard items were used for the exchange.

THE UNITED STATES OF AMERICA
FEDERAL RESERVE NOTE
100
HB 98422922 G
B2
HB 98422922 G
100
ONE HUNDRED DOLLARS
THIS NOTE IS LEGAL TENDER FOR ALL DEBTS, PUBLIC AND PRIVATE
50
FIFTY DOLLARS
20
ONE DOLLAR

Rice Grains

CATTLE AS MONEY

From 9000 to 6000 BC, cattle and other types of livestock were used around the globe as a standard form of exchange. This was a step up from barter because at this point everyone in the culture knew what the cow, or sheep, or camel represented in the exchange. As soon as farming was started, grains or grain products became a standard form of exchange as well.

COWRIE SHELLS AS MONEY

Around 1200 BC, cowrie shells began to be used for money in China. They were easy to carry and found in abundance in the Pacific and Indian Oceans. They didn't have value in and of themselves but they represented a certain value in many societies. They were still used in Africa as recently as fifty years ago.

Cowrie Shells

Ancient Chinese Coins

THE FIRST METAL MONEY AND COINS

Around 1000 BC, at the end of the era of the Stone Age, the Chinese were creating bronze as well as copper pieces in the form of cowries. They also developed money made from knives and spades. These early forms of money were a bridge from cowrie shells to primitive coins. They used base metals to make the coins and they sometimes drilled holes in their centers so they could be placed on a chain for carrying.

MODERN COINS

Around 500 BC, early coins that look more like the coins of today were created in Lydia, a region that is now part of the country of Turkey. They were made with silver and had images of gods as well as emperors stamped on them. The techniques that were developed to make these coins spread quickly to other surrounding civilizations such as the Greek, Macedonian, and Persian empires. Later on, the Romans minted coins using these techniques too. Unlike the Chinese coins, these coins had more value since they were made with gold, silver, and bronze.

Lydian Electrum Lion Coins

Ancient Chinese Banknote

LEATHER MONEY

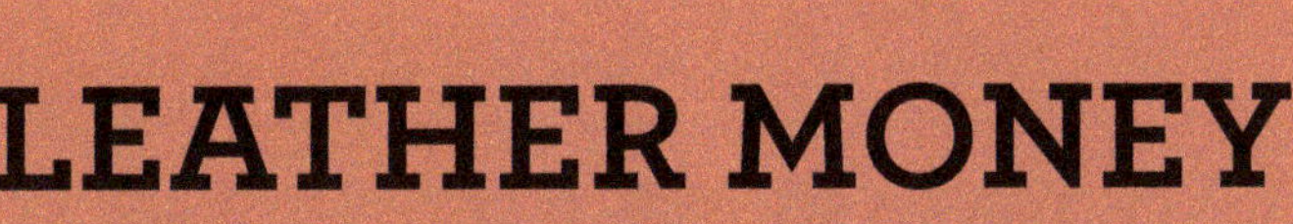

In China, around 118 BC, 1-foot square pieces of deer hide with brightly colored borders were used as the first banknotes.

PAPER MONEY IS USED IN CHINA

The Chinese were also the first civilization to use paper money beginning around 800 AD and lasting for 500 years. The only problem was that the paper money kept getting printed and its value decreased dramatically. Around 1455 AD, its use disappeared for several centuries.

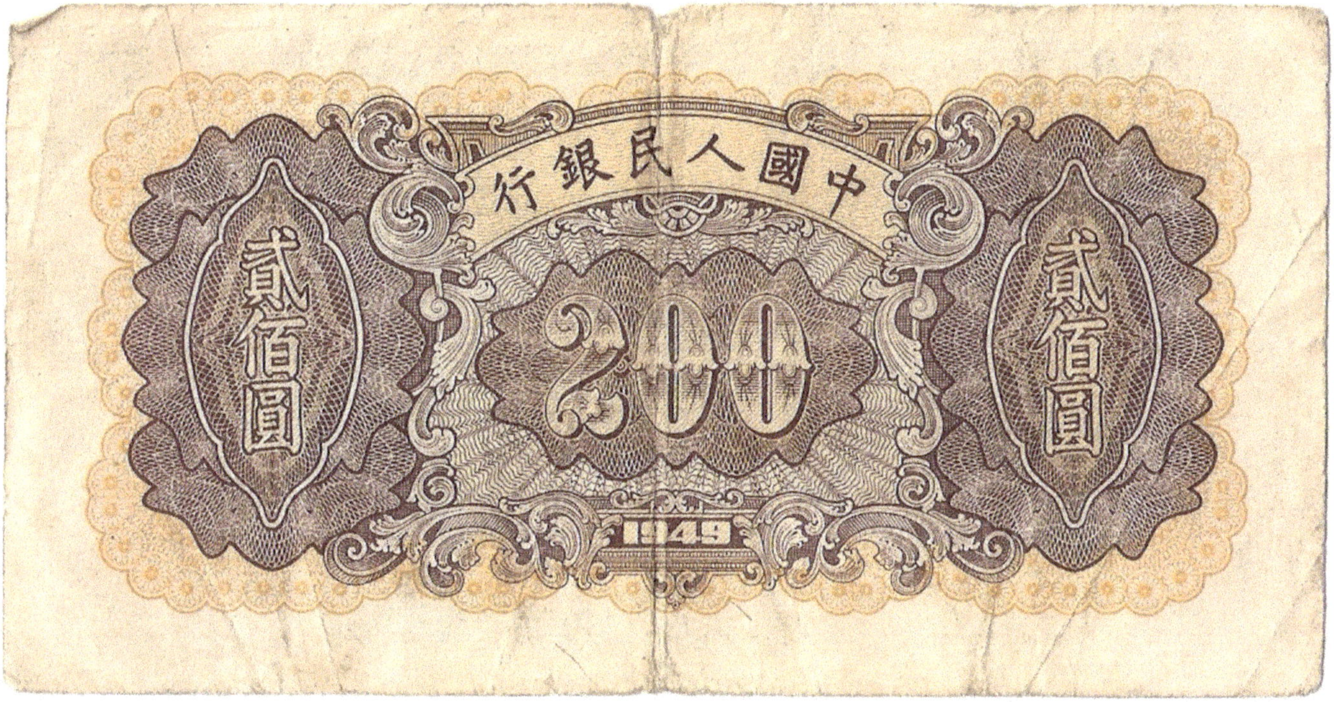

中國人民銀行

貳佰圓　200　貳佰圓

1949

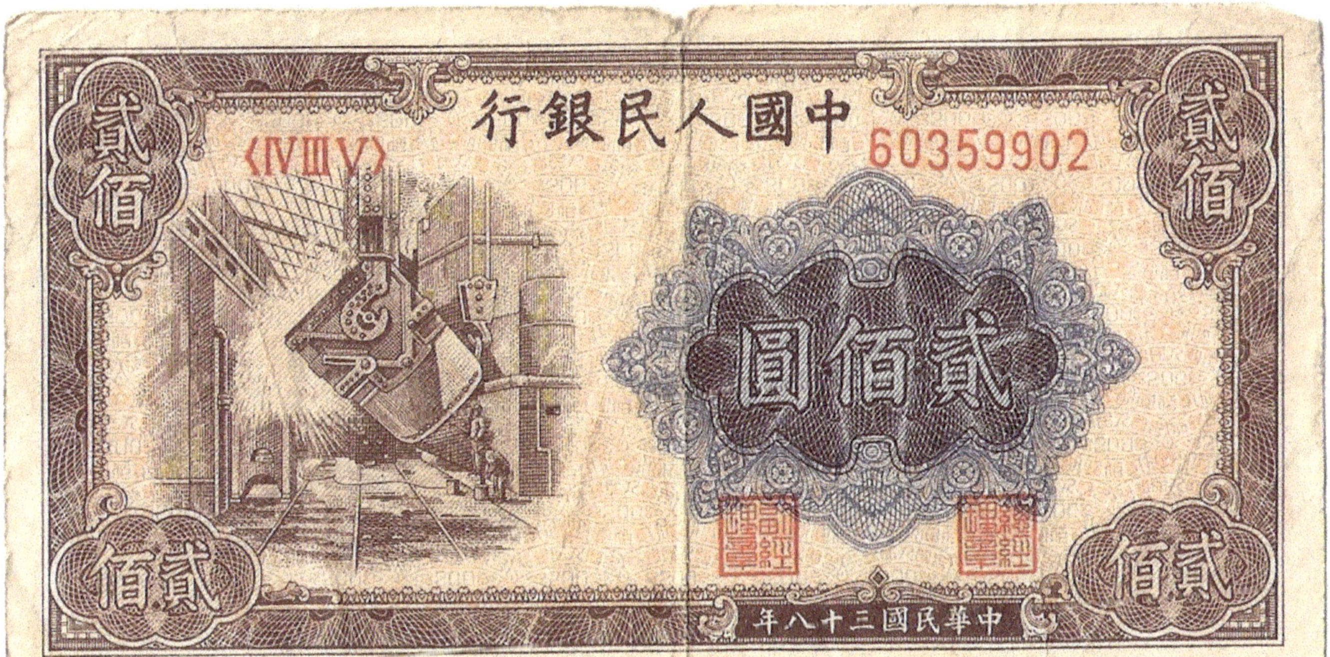

中國人民銀行

〈ⅣⅢⅤ〉　60359902

貳佰　貳佰圓　貳佰

貳佰

中華民國三十八年

18 87
REG·
·FID·
BRITT·
DEF·
Florin

THE GOLD FLORIN

Around 1250 AD, a gold coin called the florin, which was minted in Florence, Italy and used by the powerful Medici family, became widely used across Europe. The use of the florin increased commerce among European nations.

Centuries before, the idea of paper money had been introduced to Europe through The Travels of Marco Polo, but it wasn't widely accepted until 1661 AD. The first paper money was printed in Sweden. Paper money could be mass- produced without having to use precious metals. However, it could be counterfeited as well. Today, paper money has security strips woven into it to verify that it is real.

Gold Coin

THE GOLD STANDARD

England made gold its standard of value in 1816 and the United States passed the Gold Standard Act in 1900. This meant that the paper money was backed up by gold that the governments possessed.

WESTERN UNION

In 1860, Western Union began the first transfers of money by wire through the use of the telegram.

Teleprinter

Great Depression
BAKE
JOHNSON
Coca
Tobaccos

THE END OF THE GOLD STANDARD

During the Great Depression in the 1930s, the gold standard was changed and the value of gold was decreased. This was the first action taken to end the relationship between paper money and gold. President Franklin Delano Roosevelt ended the gold standard in 1933.

The credit card was invented in 1946, but it wasn't until 1959 that customers were allowed to carry a balance on their cards and not pay the total due at the end of the month.

Debit
Credit Card

Online Money Transfer

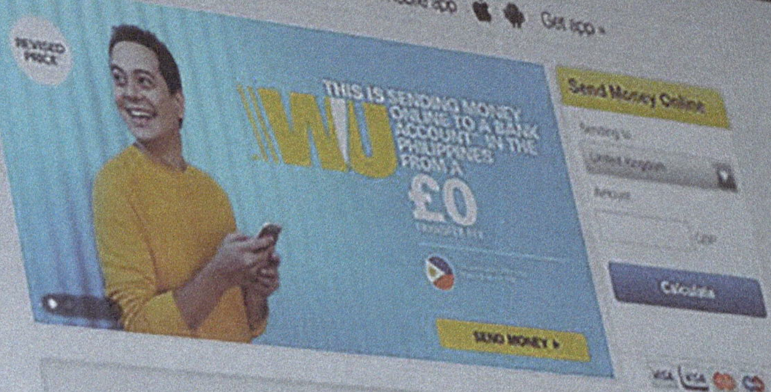

Send money on the go with our new mobile app   Get app »
REVISED PRICE
THIS IS SENDING MONEY ONLINE TO A BANK ACCOUNT IN THE PHILIPPINES FROM A
£0
TRANSFER FEE
SEND MONEY »
Send Money Online
Sending to
United Kingdom
Amount
GBP
Calculate
Bangladesh & Egypt
£0 GBP transfer fee* to send direct to a bank account in Bangladesh or Egypt
Send now
Become an Agent
Offer Western Union money transfer services from your retail location
Learn more
Fraud Awareness
Be Informed. Be Aware.
Protect yourself against fraud with awareness and education.
More about fraud protection
Send Money
Send money online
Send money in person
Send money by phone
Tools
Find locations
Track transfer
Estimate price
Legal
Intellectual property
Privacy statement
Terms & Conditions
Cookie information
Quick Links
Frequently asked questions
Contact us
Become an agent
Fraud Awareness
My Profile
Log in/Register
Connect with us
Sign up for email alerts
Email address

INNOVATIONS IN MONEY

Today we can send money back and forth without ever touching a physical piece of paper or a coin.

Suppose you wanted to pay someone who did work for you, but that person lives in another country with another form of money. Today, you can go online and pay someone $50 with a few clicks of your mouse using PayPal or some other electronic method.

50% SALE
GO•SHOP
NEW COLLECTION
UP TO 50% OFF
CHOICE COLLECTION
SHOP now
BRANDS

PayPal will transfer the money from your bank account and if you highlight the type of currency in the other country, it will pay your vendor in their country's money. Nothing will transfer from your hands to the other person's hands. It will all be done with electronic transfers on your computer or smart phone.

Bitcoin is a new type of experimental money that is transferred electronically. It works peer-to-peer so it doesn't go through a central banking system. It's value changes a lot.

FEDERAL RESERVE NOTE
THE UNITED STATES OF AMERICA
E 34112707 E
WASHINGTON, D.C.
5
ONE
SERIES 2003
John W Snow
Secretary of the Treasury.
THIS NOTE IS LEGAL TENDER
FOR ALL DEBTS, PUBLIC AND PRIVATE
ONE DOLLAR
WASHINGTON
C2
E34112707E
Rosario Marin
Treasurer of the United States.
WASHINGTON, D.C.
THE DEPARTMENT OF THE TREASURY
C 77
1

SUMMARY

Civilizations around the world began to flourish once the invention of money was instituted. At the very beginning of human society, barter was used to exchange different goods and services. Then, cattle and grain were used as a standard for bartering. Soon, money took on a more abstract form. For a time, coins were made with actual gold and silver. Leather money and paper money followed. Then, the concept of buying something over time in installments and credit cards were introduced. Today, electronic forms of money are making it possible for people to buy and sell online without exchanging anything from hand to hand.

Awesome! Now that you know more about why we use money and how technology has changed money, you can read about how modern coins are minted in the Baby Professor book How Do They Do It? Coins Edition.

Visit
BABY PROFESSOR
EDUCATION KIDS
www.BabyProfessorBooks.com
to download Free Baby Professor eBooks
and view our catalog of new and exciting
Children's Books